The Ultima

Anti Inflammatory

Air Fryer Cookbook

Elevate Your Health With Air Fried Anti-Inflammatory Goodness

JAMES AUSTIN

Table Of Content

-Chicken Stir-Fry with Broccoli and Cashews
-Lentil and Vegetable Curry
-Grilled Chicken and Avocado Salad
-Quinoa and Kale Buddha Bowl
-Zucchini Noodles with Pesto and Cherry Tomatoes
-Lentil and Vegetable Soup
-Salmon and Avocado Nori Rolls
-Mediterranean Quinoa Salad
-Spinach and Chickpea Stuffed Sweet Potato
-Grilled Vegetable Wrap
-Lentil and Roasted Vegetable Salad
-Cucumber Avocado Gazpacho
-Thai-Inspired Quinoa Salad
-Caprese Chickpea Salad
-Asian-style Tofu and Vegetable Stir-Fry

CHAPTER 4
SNACKS
-Turmeric Roasted Chickpeas
-Avocado and Cucumber Salsa
-Baked Sweet Potato Chips
-Zucchini and Carrot FrittersGrilled Shrimp Tacos
with Avocado Lime Crema
-Berry Chia Seed Pudding
-Grilled Shrimp Tacos with Avocado Lime Crema
-Almond Butter Energy Bites
-Cucumber and Hummus Bites
-Roasted Red Pepper and Walnut Dip
-Chia Seed and Mixed Berry Smoothie

CHAPTER 7
DESSERTS
-Berry Chia Seed Pudding
-Baked Cinnamon Apples
-Turmeric Ginger Cookies
-Avocado Chocolate Mousse
-Almond Butter and Banana Bites
-Coconut Blueberry Popsicles
-Mango Turmeric Sorbet
-Cinnamon Baked Pears
Recipe Index
CONCLUSION

Introduction

In our fast-paced, modern world, the pursuit of better health and wellness has become a paramount goal for many individuals. As we navigate the complexities of our daily lives, we are increasingly realizing the profound impact that our diet and lifestyle choices have on our overall well-being. The rising prevalence of chronic diseases, autoimmune disorders, and other health challenges has prompted us to explore alternative approaches to nutrition and explore how our dietary habits can either support or hinder our journey to optimal health.

This book delves into the fascinating realm of the inflammatory diet, a concept that has garnered significant attention in recent years due to its potential to positively influence our health and vitality. At its core, the inflammatory diet centers on the idea that certain foods have the power to trigger inflammation in the body, which can lead to a myriad of health issues.

Inflammation is a natural response by our immune system to protect us from harmful stimuli such as pathogens, injuries, and toxins. However, when inflammation becomes chronic and prolonged, it can wreak havoc on our organs, tissues, and cells, contributing to the development of various diseases, including cardiovascular conditions, diabetes, arthritis, and even certain cancers. Fortunately, through conscious dietary choices, we have the ability to modulate inflammation and promote healing within our bodies.

The primary goal of this book is to provide you with a comprehensive understanding of the inflammatory diet and how it can revolutionize your approach to nutrition. Through an evidence-based exploration of various foods, their inflammatory potential, and their impact on our overall health, we aim to empower you to make informed decisions about what you eat, leading you towards a healthier, more vibrant life.

In the following chapters, we will embark on a journey to uncover the fundamental principles of the inflammatory diet, debunking common misconceptions, and presenting you with cutting-edge research to support our claims. Additionally, we will delve into practical tips and strategies for implementing an anti-inflammatory lifestyle into your daily routine, offering guidance on meal planning, cooking techniques, and mindful eating practices.

Furthermore, we recognize that each person's body is unique, and what works for one may not work for another. As such, we encourage you to approach the information within this book with an open mind and a willingness to experiment with your diet to find what resonates best with your individual needs and preferences.

Whether you are a seasoned health enthusiast or new to the concept of the inflammatory diet, we hope that this book will serve as a valuable resource on your path to better health and well-being. By understanding the intricate relationship between the foods we consume and their impact on our bodies, we can take control of our health and foster a harmonious balance between nutrition and inflammation.

Join us on this transformative journey as we embrace the power of the inflammatory diet and unlock the potential for a healthier, happier, and more vibrant life. Together, we will embark on a holistic approach to wellness that nourishes not only our bodies but also our minds and spirits, enabling us to live life to its fullest potential. Let us embrace the wisdom of our ancestors, the advancements of modern science, and the innate intelligence of our bodies as we step into the realm of the inflammatory diet

Symptoms Of inflammation

The symptoms of inflammation can vary depending on the affected area of the body, but common symptoms include.

Redness: The affected area may become red due to increased blood flow to the site of inflammation.

Swelling: Inflammation often causes fluid to accumulate in the affected area, leading to swelling.

Heat: Increased blood flow can also cause the affected area to feel warm or hot to the touch.

Pain: Inflammation can trigger the release of chemicals that stimulate nerve endings, leading to pain or discomfort.

Loss of function: In some cases, inflammation can affect the function of the affected body part, leading to limitations in movement or reduced functionality.

Fatigue: Systemic inflammation (affecting the whole body) can lead to a general feeling of fatigue and malaise.

Fever: Infections or severe inflammation may cause a fever as part of the body's defense mechanism.

Headache: Inflammation involving the brain or its surrounding structures can lead to headaches.

Joint stiffness: Inflammation in joints can cause stiffness and reduced range of motion.

Rash or skin changes: Inflammatory skin conditions may lead to rashes, itching, or changes in the skin's appearance.

Diseases Due To Inflammation

Some diseases that can be caused or exacerbated by inflammation include

Rheumatoid arthritis: An autoimmune disease where the immune system attacks the joints, leading to chronic inflammation, pain, and joint damage.

Osteoarthritis: A degenerative joint disease where the cartilage that cushions the ends of bones wears down, leading to inflammation, pain, and stiffness.

Inflammatory Bowel Disease (IBD): Including Crohn's disease and ulcerative colitis, these are chronic inflammatory conditions that affect the gastrointestinal tract, leading to symptoms like abdominal pain, diarrhea, and weight loss.

Asthma: An inflammatory disorder of the airways that can cause breathing difficulties, wheezing, and coughing.

Chronic obstructive pulmonary disease (COPD): A group of lung diseases, including chronic bronchitis and emphysema, which involve chronic inflammation in the airways and lungs, leading to breathing difficulties.

Cardiovascular diseases: Chronic inflammation is believed to play a role in the development of atherosclerosis (hardening and narrowing of the arteries), leading to conditions like coronary artery disease, heart attacks, and strokes.

Diabetes: Chronic inflammation may contribute to insulin resistance and other complications associated with both type 1 and type 2 diabetes.

Psoriasis: A skin condition characterized by patches of red, inflamed skin covered with silvery scales, resulting from an overactive immune response.

Eczema: Also known as atopic dermatitis, it is a chronic skin condition characterized by inflamed, itchy skin.

Alzheimer's disease: Chronic inflammation in the brain is thought to play a role in the development and progression of Alzheimer's disease.

Cancer: Chronic inflammation can promote cellular damage and mutations, increasing the risk of cancer development.

Benefits of the Anti-Inflammatory Diet for Optimal Health

The Anti-Inflammatory Diet is a nutritional approach designed to reduce inflammation in the body, which is linked to various chronic diseases and health issues. By incorporating specific foods and avoiding inflammatory triggers, this diet offers a wide range of benefits that can contribute to your overall well-being. Here are some of the key advantages you can expect from following an Anti-Inflammatory Diet.

Reduced Chronic Inflammation: The Anti-Inflammatory Diet's main objective is to fight chronic inflammation. By choosing foods that are rich in antioxidants, omega-3 fatty acids, and other anti-inflammatory compounds, you can lower the levels of pro-inflammatory markers in your body, leading to decreased inflammation.

Improved Joint Health: Many inflammatory conditions affect the joints, such as rheumatoid arthritis and osteoarthritis. By following this diet, you may experience reduced joint pain and stiffness, as inflammation is minimized, providing relief and improved mobility.

Heart Health: The Anti-Inflammatory Diet promotes heart health by encouraging the consumption of heart-friendly foods like fruits, vegetables, whole grains, and healthy fats. These choices can help lower cholesterol levels, blood pressure, and reduce the risk of heart disease.

Weight Management: The diet emphasizes whole, nutrient-dense foods while limiting processed and sugary items. This approach can help with weight management and weight loss, as you naturally reduce calorie intake and make healthier food choices.

Balanced Blood Sugar Levels: By avoiding refined carbohydrates and sugar-laden foods, the Anti-Inflammatory Diet can help regulate blood sugar levels, reducing the risk of insulin resistance and type 2 diabetes.

Enhanced Gut Health: A healthy gut is crucial for overall well-being, and the Anti-Inflammatory Diet promotes a diverse range of gut-friendly foods, including probiotics and fiber-rich options. These foods can support a balanced gut microbiome, aiding in digestion and overall gut health.

Boosted Immune System: The diet's focus on nutrient-rich foods strengthens the immune system, making your body better equipped to fend off infections and illnesses.

Clearer Skin: Inflammatory foods can sometimes trigger skin conditions like acne and eczema. By removing such triggers and incorporating foods that promote skin health, the Anti-Inflammatory Diet may lead to clearer, more radiant skin.

Improved Cognitive Function: Chronic inflammation has been linked to cognitive decline and neurological disorders. By reducing inflammation through the Anti-Inflammatory Diet, you may support better brain health and cognitive function.

Reduced Risk of Chronic Diseases: Overall, by adopting this diet, you can reduce your risk of various chronic diseases, including certain cancers, Alzheimer's disease, and autoimmune disorders, thanks to the diet's anti-inflammatory properties.

What Is Inflammatory Diet

An inflammatory diet is one that can contribute to chronic inflammation in the body, which has been linked to various health issues such as heart disease, diabetes, arthritis, and certain types of cancer.

Adopting an anti-inflammatory diet can help reduce inflammation and promote overall health. Here are some general guidelines on what to eat and what to avoid in an anti-inflammatory diet:

Foods to Eat in an Anti-Inflammatory Diet

1. **Fruits:** Berries (blueberries, strawberries, raspberries), cherries, oranges, kiwi, and other fruits rich in antioxidants and vitamins.
2. **Vegetables:** Leafy greens (spinach, kale, collard greens), broccoli, cauliflower, carrots, sweet potatoes, and other colorful vegetables high in nutrients and fiber.
3. **Healthy Fats:** Avocado, olive oil (extra virgin), nuts (almonds, walnuts), and seeds (chia, flaxseed) provide beneficial monounsaturated and polyunsaturated fats.

4. **Fatty Fish:** Salmon, mackerel, sardines, and trout are rich in omega-3 fatty acids, known for their anti-inflammatory properties.

5. **Whole Grains:** Brown rice, quinoa, oats, and whole wheat, which are a good source of fiber and nutrients.

6. **Legumes:** Lentils, chickpeas, black beans, and other legumes offer protein and fiber.

7. **Herbs and Spices:** Turmeric, ginger, garlic, cinnamon, and rosemary have anti-inflammatory properties.

8. **Green Tea:** Rich in antioxidants, green tea can help reduce inflammation.

Foods to Avoid or Limit

1. **Processed Foods:** Highly processed and packaged foods often contain unhealthy fats, added sugars, and artificial additives that can promote inflammation.

2. **Sugary Beverages**: Soda, sweetened juices, and energy drinks are high in added sugars, which can contribute to inflammation.

3. **Trans Fats:** Found in hydrogenated oils and many fried and commercially baked goods, trans fats are known to promote inflammation and should be avoided.

4. **Red Meat:** High red meat consumption has been linked to an increase in inflammation. Opt for leaner protein sources or plant-based alternatives.

5. **Refined Carbohydrates:** White bread, white rice, and other refined grains can cause spikes in blood sugar and contribute to inflammation.

6. **Excessive Alcohol:** While moderate alcohol consumption may have some health benefits, excessive drinking can lead to inflammation and other health issues.

CHAPTER 1

ANTI INFLAMMATORY RECIPES

Breakfast Recipe
Turmeric Chia Seed Pudding

Ingredients:

- 1 cup almond milk (or other plant-based milk) that hasn't been sweetened
- 3 tablespoons chia seeds
- 1 teaspoon ground turmeric
- 1/2 teaspoon ground cinnamon
- 1/4 teaspoon ground ginger
- 1/2 teaspoon vanilla extract
- 1 tablespoon honey or maple syrup (optional)

- Fresh berries for topping

Instructions:

1. In a bowl, whisk together the almond milk, chia seeds, turmeric, cinnamon, ginger, and vanilla extract.
2. Sweeten with honey or maple syrup, if preferred.
3. In order for the chia seeds to absorb the liquid and thicken, the dish has to be covered and chilled for at least 4 hours or overnight.
4. Before serving, give it a good stir and top with fresh berries.

Avocado and Smoked Salmon Toast

Ingredients:

- 2 slices whole-grain or gluten-free bread
- 1 ripe avocado, mashed
- Juice of half a lemon
- 1/4 teaspoon red pepper flakes (optional)
- 4-6 ounces smoked salmon
- Fresh dill, for garnish
- Salt and pepper to taste

Instructions:

1. Toast the bread slices to your desired level of crispness.
2. In a bowl, mash the avocado and mix it with lemon juice, red pepper flakes (if using), salt, and pepper.
3. Spread the avocado mixture evenly onto the toasted bread slices.
4. Top each toast with smoked salmon and garnish with fresh dill.

Berry Spinach Smoothie

Ingredients:

- 1 cup fresh or frozen mixed berries (blueberries, strawberries, raspberries)
- 1 cup baby spinach leaves
- 1 ripe banana
- 1 tablespoon chia seeds
- 1 cup almond milk (or other plant-based milk) that hasn't been sweetened
- Greek yogurt plain, 1/2 cup (optional; for richness).
- 1 teaspoon of optionally added sweetness, such as honey or agave syrup
- Instructions:
- Blend each item in the blender until completely smooth and creamy.
- Use honey or agave syrup to taste and, if required, adjust sweetness.

- Enjoy the antioxidant boost by pouring the smoothie into a glass.

Quinoa Breakfast Bowl

Ingredients:

- Ingredients:
- cooked quinoa, 1 cup
- coconut milk, or any other plant-based milk, in 1/2 cup
- 1 tablespoon almond butter
- 1 tablespoon unsweetened shredded coconut
- 1/4 cup fresh mixed berries
- 1 tablespoon chopped almonds or walnuts
- 1 teaspoon honey (optional)

Instructions:

1. In a saucepan, warm the coconut milk and stir in the almond butter until smooth.
2. Add the cooked quinoa to the saucepan and mix well, ensuring it's evenly coated with the almond-coconut mixture.
3. Transfer the quinoa to a bowl and top with shredded coconut, mixed berries, chopped almonds or walnuts, and a drizzle of honey if desired.

Golden Breakfast Oatmeal

Ingredients:

- 1 cup rolled oats (gluten-free if required)
1. 2 cups of your choice of water or milk
2. 1 teaspoon of turmeric, ground
3. 1/8 teaspoon cinnamon powder
4. 1/8 teaspoon of ginger powder
5. Pinch of black pepper (to increase the health benefits of turmeric)

6. 1 tablespoon maple syrup or honey (optional)
7. Apple or banana slices for the topping
8. Instructions:
9. Oats, water or milk, turmeric, cinnamon, ginger, and black pepper should all be combined in a pot.
10. Cook the oats until they are soft and creamy over medium heat, stirring periodically.
11. Oatmeal should be served in bowls with chopped apple or banana on top.
12. Serve the oatmeal in bowls and top with sliced banana or diced apple.

Sweet Potato and Kale Frittata

Ingredients:

- 6 large eggs
- 1 medium sweet potato, finely sliced after being peeled

- 1 cup chopped kale (stems removed)
- 1/2 cup diced red bell pepper
- 1/4 cup chopped green onions
- 1/4 teaspoon turmeric powder
- 1/4 teaspoon garlic powder
- Salt and pepper to taste
- 1 tablespoon olive oil

Instructions:

1. Preheat your oven to 375°F (190°C).
2. The olive oil should be heated over medium heat in a large oven-safe pan.
3. Sliced sweet potatoes are added, and they are cooked for approximately 5 minutes, or until they begin to soften.
4. Add the green onions, red bell pepper, and chopped kale. Cook the veggies for a further 2 minutes, or until they are just soft.
5. Whisk the eggs with the garlic powder, turmeric, salt, and pepper in a bowl.

6. Over the veggies in the skillet, evenly pour the egg mixture.

7. Cook for 2 minutes on the stovetop, then transfer the skillet to the preheated oven.

8. Bake for 12-15 minutes or until the frittata is set and lightly golden on top.

9. Slice and serve warm.

Mango Coconut Chia Pudding

Ingredients:

- 1 ripe mango, peeled and pitted
1. Coconut milk, or any other plant-based milk, in a cup
2. three cups of chia seeds
3. One-half teaspoon of vanilla extract
4. 1 tablespoon of unsweetened coconut shreds
5. mint leaves for garnish, fresh
6. Instructions:

7. Mangoes should be pureed in a blender until smooth.

8. In a bowl, combine the mango puree, coconut milk, chia seeds, and vanilla extract. Mix well.

9. To enable the chia seeds to thicken, cover the bowl and place it in the refrigerator for at least two hours or overnight.

Apple Cinnamon Quinoa Breakfast Bowl

Ingredients:

- 1 cup cooked quinoa
- 1 apple, diced
- 1/4 cup chopped walnuts or almonds
- 1/2 teaspoon ground cinnamon
- 1 tablespoon pure maple syrup
- 1/4 cup unsweetened almond milk (or any plant-based milk)

- Pinch of salt

Instructions:

1. Warm the cooked quinoa and almond milk in a saucepan over medium heat.
2. Stir in the diced apple, chopped walnuts or almonds, ground cinnamon, maple syrup, and a pinch of salt.
3. Cook for a few minutes until the apple softens and the mixture is heated through.
4. Serve the quinoa breakfast bowl warm.

Green Smoothie Bowl

Ingredients:

- 1 cup fresh spinach leaves
- 1 ripe banana
- 1/2 cup diced pineapple (fresh or frozen)

- 1/2 cup diced cucumber
- 1/2 cup unsweetened coconut water (or any plant-based milk)
- 1 tablespoon chia seeds
- Toppings: sliced kiwi, shredded coconut, sliced almonds, chia seeds

Instructions:

1. In a blender, combine the spinach, banana, pineapple, cucumber, coconut water, and chia seeds.
2. Blend until smooth and creamy.
3. Pour the green smoothie into a bowl and add your favorite toppings.

Almond Butter and Blueberry Overnight Oats

Ingredients:

- 1 cup rolled oats (gluten-free if required)
- 1 cup almond milk (or other plant-based milk) that hasn't been sweetened
- Almond butter, two teaspoons
- fresh blueberries, half a cup
- 1 tablespoon honey or maple syrup (optional, for added sweetness)

Instructions:

1. In a jar or container, mix the oats, almond milk, and almond butter until well combined.
2. Stir in the fresh blueberries and sweeten with honey or maple syrup if desired.
3. Cover the jar and refrigerate overnight.
4. In the morning, give the oats a good stir and enjoy them cold or slightly warmed.

Spinach and Mushroom Egg Muffins

Ingredients:

- 6 large eggs
- 1 cup fresh baby spinach, chopped
- 1 cup sliced mushrooms
- 1/2 cup diced red bell pepper
- 1/4 cup chopped green onions
- 1/4 teaspoon turmeric powder
- Salt and pepper to taste
- Olive oil or cooking spray for greasing

Instructions:

1. Preheat your oven to 375°F (190°C) and lightly grease a muffin tin with olive oil or cooking spray.

2. Whisk the eggs with the turmeric, salt, and pepper in a bowl.

3. Add the spinach, mushrooms, red bell pepper, and green onions, all diced.

4. The egg mixture should be poured into each muffin cup until it is about two thirds filled.

5. Bake the egg muffins for 15 to 18 minutes, or until they are set and have a light golden brown top.

6. Before removing them from the muffin tray, let them cool somewhat.

7. Enjoy these savory egg muffins for a quick and nutritious breakfast on the go.

Coconut Berry Oat Bars

Ingredients:

- 1 1/2 cups rolled oats (gluten-free if required)
- 1 cup shredded unsweetened coconut

- 1/2 cup almond flour
- 1/4 cup coconut oil, melted
- 1/4 cup pure maple syrup
- 1 teaspoon vanilla extract
- Blueberries, raspberries, or strawberries make up half a cup of mixed berries.

Instructions:

1. Preheat your oven to 350°F (175°C) and line an 8x8-inch baking dish with parchment paper.
2. In a large bowl, mix together the rolled oats, shredded coconut, and almond flour.
3. Stir in the melted coconut oil, maple syrup, and vanilla extract until well combined.
4. Press about two-thirds of the mixture into the prepared baking dish to form a crust.
5. Over the crust, equally distribute the mixed berries.
6. As a crumble topping, scatter the leftover oat mixture over the berries.

7. Bake for 20 to 25 minutes, or until the edges are lightly browned.

8. Before cutting the bars into squares, let the bars totally cool.

Peanut Butter Banana Smoothie

Ingredients:

- 1 ripe banana
- 2 tablespoons natural peanut butter
- 1 cup almond milk that hasn't been sweetened
- 1 tablespoon flax seeds
- 1/2 teaspoon ground cinnamon
- Ice cubes (optional)

Instructions:

1. In a blender, combine the ripe banana, peanut butter, almond milk, flaxseeds, and ground cinnamon.
2. Blend until smooth and creamy.
3. Add ice cubes if desired and blend again for a colder and thicker texture.
4. Pour the peanut butter banana smoothie into a glass and enjoy!

Anti-Inflammatory Tropical Smoothie

Ingredients:

- 1 cup diced pineapple (fresh or frozen)
- 1/2 cup diced mango (fresh or frozen)
- 1/2 cup diced papaya (fresh or frozen)
- 1 orange, peeled and segmented
- 1/2 teaspoon grated fresh ginger
- 1/2 cup coconut water (or any plant-based milk)

- 1 tablespoon hemp seeds (optional, for added nutrition)

Instructions:

1. In a blender, combine the pineapple, mango, papaya, orange segments, grated ginger, and coconut water.
2. Blend until smooth and creamy.
3. Add hemp seeds if desired and blend again for an extra boost of nutrients.
4. Pour the tropical smoothie into a glass and enjoy the refreshing flavors

Blueberry Almond Chia Pudding

Ingredients:

- a single serving of unsweetened almond milk (or other plant-based milk)

- 1/4 cup chia seeds
- 1/2 teaspoon vanilla extract
- 1 tablespoon almond butter
- 1 cup fresh blueberries
- 1 tablespoon slivered almonds

Instructions:

1. In a jar or container, mix the almond milk, chia seeds, vanilla extract, and almond butter.
2. Stir well and refrigerate overnight or for at least 2 hours until the chia seeds thicken.
3. Before serving, top the chia pudding with fresh blueberries and slivered almonds.

Mediterranean Veggie Omelette

Ingredients:

- 3 large eggs
- 2 tablespoons water or milk of your choice
- 1/4 cup diced tomatoes
- 1/4 cup diced bell peppers (any color)
- 1/4 cup chopped baby spinach
- 2 tablespoons diced red onion
- 2 tablespoons crumbled feta cheese
- 1 tablespoon chopped fresh parsley
- Salt and pepper to taste
- Olive oil for cooking

Instructions:

Olive oil should be warmed up over medium heat in a nonstick pan.

Red onion, bell peppers, and diced tomatoes should all be added. Several minutes of sautéing will soften.

Over the sautéed veggies in the skillet, pour the whisked eggs.

Lift the edges once the eggs have set to allow the uncooked egg to flow below while cooking.

Over one side of the omelet, top with feta cheese, fresh parsley, and chopped spinach.

When the cheese has melted, fold the second half of the omelet over the contents and cook for one more minute.

Serve the omelet hot after sliding it onto a dish.

CHAPTER 2

LUNCH RECIPES

Embracing an anti-inflammatory diet can do wonders for your overall health and well-being. By incorporating ingredients that combat inflammation, you can promote a balanced immune system, reduce the risk of chronic diseases, and boost your energy levels. Here, we present a selection of delicious and nutrient-packed lunch recipes to help you stay on track with your anti-inflammatory journey.

Quinoa and Roasted Vegetable Salad

Ingredients:

- 1 cup quinoa, rinsed

- 2 cups mixed vegetables (bell peppers, zucchini, cherry tomatoes, red onion)
- 2 tablespoons olive oil
- 1 teaspoon dried oregano
- 1/2 teaspoon garlic powder
- Salt and pepper to taste
- 2 cups baby spinach
- 1/4 cup chopped fresh basil
- 1/4 cup crumbled feta cheese (optional)

Instructions:

1. Preheat your oven to 425°F (220°C).
2. Combine the olive oil, dried oregano, garlic powder, salt, and pepper with the mixed veggies. They should be spread out on a baking sheet and roasted for 20 to 25 minutes, or until soft and just browned.
3. Meanwhile, cook quinoa according to package instructions.

4. In a large bowl, combine cooked quinoa, roasted vegetables, baby spinach, and fresh basil. Toss gently to mix.
5. If desired, sprinkle crumbled feta cheese on top. Serve warm or at room temperature.

Turmeric Ginger Carrot Soup

Ingredients:

- 1 tablespoon coconut oil
- 1 large onion, chopped
- 3 cloves garlic, minced
- 1 tablespoon grated fresh ginger
- 1 lb (450g) carrots, peeled and chopped
- 1 teaspoon ground turmeric
- 4 cups vegetable broth
- 1 can (13.5 oz) coconut milk
- Salt and pepper to taste
- Fresh cilantro or parsley for garnish

Instructions:

1. Coconut oil should be heated in a big saucepan over a medium heat. Add the ground turmeric, ginger, and garlic, all minced. one more minute of cooking.
2. Vegetable broth and diced carrots should be added to the saucepan. When the carrots are ready, simmer for 15 to 20 minutes after bringing to a boil.
3. Puree the soup using an immersion blender until it's smooth.Alternatively, transfer the soup in batches to a regular blender and blend until smooth, being careful not to fill the blender jar too full with hot liquid.
4. Return the pureed soup to the pot, stir in coconut milk, and season with salt and pepper to taste.
5. Heat the soup gently for a few more minutes, but do not let it boil.
6. Ladle the soup into bowls, garnish with fresh cilantro or parsley, and serve hot.

Salmon Avocado Lettuce Wraps

Ingredients:

- 2 large lettuce leaves (butter lettuce or romaine work well)
- 6 oz (170g) cooked salmon, flaked
- 1 ripe avocado, sliced
- 1/2 cucumber, thinly sliced
- 1/4 red onion, thinly sliced
- 1 tablespoon lemon juice
- 1 tablespoon olive oil
- Salt and pepper to taste
- Optional: Fresh dill or cilantro for extra flavor

Instructions:

1. In a small bowl, combine lemon juice, olive oil, salt, and pepper to make the dressing.

2. Lay the lettuce leaves flat and divide the flaked salmon evenly between them.
3. Top the salmon with avocado slices, cucumber slices, and red onion.
4. Drizzle the dressing over the fillings and add fresh dill or cilantro if desired.
5. Wrap the lettuce leaves around the fillings, creating neat wraps. Enjoy these refreshing and nutritious salmon avocado lettuce wraps!

Grilled Vegetable Quinoa Bowl

Ingredients:

- 1 cup quinoa, rinsed
- 2 cups mixed vegetables (asparagus, eggplant, bell peppers, cherry tomatoes)
- 2 tablespoons balsamic vinegar
- 2 tablespoons olive oil
- 1 teaspoon dried thyme

- Salt and pepper to taste
- 1/4 cup toasted pine nuts
- Fresh basil leaves for garnish

Instructions:

1. Cook quinoa according to package instructions.
2. In a bowl, toss the mixed vegetables with balsamic vinegar, olive oil, dried thyme, salt, and pepper.
3. Grill the vegetables for about 5-7 minutes, or until they are tender and have grill marks.
4. In a serving bowl, layer the cooked quinoa, grilled vegetables, and toasted pine nuts.
5. Garnish with fresh basil leaves before serving.

Chickpea and Spinach Salad

Ingredients:

- 1 can (15 oz) washed and drained chickpeas
- 2 cups baby spinach leaves
- 1 cup cherry tomatoes, halved
- 1/2 cucumber, diced
- 1/4 red onion, thinly sliced
- 2 tablespoons lemon juice
- 2 tablespoons extra-virgin olive oil
- 1 teaspoon ground cumin
- 1/2 teaspoon paprika
- Salt and pepper to taste
- Optional: crumbled feta cheese or avocado slices for added creaminess

Instructions:

1. In a large salad bowl, combine chickpeas, baby spinach, cherry tomatoes, cucumber, and red onion.
2. In a separate small bowl, whisk together lemon juice, olive oil, ground cumin, paprika, salt, and pepper to make the dressing.

3. Drizzle the salad with the dressing and toss to combine.

4. If desired, add crumbled feta cheese or avocado slices on top before serving.

Lentil and Vegetable Stir-Fry

Ingredients:

- 1 cup cooked green lentils
- 1 cup broccoli florets
- 1 cup sliced bell peppers (mixed colors)
- 1 cup sliced carrots
- 1 cup snap peas
- 2 teaspoons soy sauce (or tamari if you're gluten-free)
- 1 tablespoon sesame oil
- 1 tablespoon rice vinegar
- 1 teaspoon grated fresh ginger
- 2 cloves garlic, minced
- 1 tablespoon sesame seeds (optional)

- Green onions, chopped, for garnish

Instructions:

1. Sesame oil should be heated over medium-high heat in a large wok or pan.
2. Stir-fry the grated ginger and minced garlic for one minute, or until fragrant.
3. Add the bell peppers and carrot slices to the pan. Stir-fry until slightly softened for 2 to 3 minutes.
4. Once the veggies are crisp-tender, add the broccoli florets and snap peas and stir-fry for an additional 2-3 minutes.
5. Soy sauce and the cooked green lentils should be combined. Combine everything and stir until well hot.
6.
7. Remove from heat, drizzle with rice vinegar, and sprinkle sesame seeds on top for extra crunch and flavor.

8. Garnish with chopped green onions before serving.

Grilled Lemon Herb Chicken Salad

Ingredients:

- 2 boneless, skinless chicken breasts
- 2 tablespoons olive oil
- 2 tablespoons fresh lemon juice
- 1 teaspoon dried oregano
- 1 teaspoon dried thyme
- Salt and pepper to taste
- 4 cups mixed salad greens (spinach, arugula, or kale)
- 1 cup cherry tomatoes, halved
- 1/2 cucumber, sliced
- 1/4 cup sliced red onion
- 1/4 cup Kalamata olives
- Crumbled feta cheese (optional)

Instructions:

1. In a bowl, whisk together olive oil, lemon juice, dried oregano, dried thyme, salt, and pepper to make the marinade.

2. Put the chicken breasts in a shallow dish or resealable plastic bag and cover them with the marinade. For at least 30 minutes (or more for extra flavor), cover the dish with plastic wrap or a sealable bag and marinate it in the fridge.

3. Over medium-high heat, preheat a grill or grill pan. The chicken should be taken out of the marinade and grilled for 6 to 8 minutes on each side, or until fully cooked.

4. Before slicing the chicken, give it some time to rest.

5. In a large salad bowl, combine the mixed salad greens, cherry tomatoes, cucumber, red onion, and Kalamata olives.

6. Top the salad with sliced grilled chicken and optional crumbled feta cheese.

7. Drizzle with additional lemon juice or olive oil if desired and toss everything together before serving.

Sweet Potato and Black Bean Tacos

Ingredients:

- 2 large sweet potatoes, peeled and cubed
- 2 tablespoons olive oil
- 1 teaspoon ground cumin
- 1 teaspoon chili powder
- Salt and pepper to taste
- 1 can (15 oz) washed and drained black beans
- 1 cup shredded red cabbage
- 1 avocado, sliced
- Fresh cilantro leaves
- Corn tortillas (or gluten-free tortillas)

Instructions:

1. Preheat your oven to 425°F (220°C).
2. In a bowl, toss the sweet potato cubes with olive oil, ground cumin, chili powder, salt, and pepper.
3. Spread the seasoned sweet potatoes on a baking sheet and roast for about 20-25 minutes or until they are tender and lightly browned.
4. In a small pan over low heat, reheat the black beans.
5. Assemble the tacos by filling each corn tortilla with roasted sweet potatoes, warmed black beans, shredded red cabbage, sliced avocado, and fresh cilantro leaves.
6. Serve the tacos warm and enjoy their satisfying combination of flavors and textures.

Roasted Vegetable and Chickpea Buddha Bowl

Ingredients:

- 1 cup cooked quinoa or brown rice
- chickpeas, drained and rinsed, from one can (15 oz).
- 2 cups mixed vegetables (cauliflower, sweet potatoes, Brussels sprouts)
- 2 tablespoons olive oil
- 1 teaspoon ground cumin
- 1/2 teaspoon smoked paprika
- Salt and pepper to taste
- 2 cups baby spinach or kale
- Lemon-tahini dressing (1/4 cup tahini, 2 tablespoons lemon juice, 2 tablespoons water, 1 clove garlic, salt, and pepper)

Instructions:

1. Preheat your oven to 425°F (220°C).

2. Toss the mixed vegetables with olive oil, ground cumin, smoked paprika, salt, and pepper. Spread them Roast for 20–25 minutes, or until fork-tender and gently browned, on a baking sheet.

3. In a large bowl, assemble the Buddha bowl by layering cooked quinoa or brown rice, roasted vegetables, chickpeas, and baby spinach or kale.

4. Drizzle the lemon-tahini dressing over the bowl and serve warm or at room temperature

Thai Coconut Curry with Tofu and Vegetables

Ingredients:

- 1 tablespoon coconut oil
- 1 block of firm tofu, cubed

- 1 tablespoon Thai red curry paste
- 1 can (13.5 oz) coconut milk
- 1 cup sliced bell peppers (mixed colors)
- 1 cup sliced zucchini
- 1 cup sliced mushrooms
- 1 cup baby corn, halved
- 1 tablespoon soy sauce (or tamari for gluten-free option)
- 1 tablespoon lime juice
- Fresh cilantro and sliced red chili for garnish (optional)
- Cooked brown rice or quinoa for serving

Instructions:

1. Heat the coconut oil over medium-high heat in a big skillet or wok.
2. Cubed tofu should be added and stir-fried until golden and slightly crispy. From the skillet, take out the tofu, and set it aside.
3. In the same skillet, add Thai red curry paste and cook for a minute to release its flavors.

4. Pour in the coconut milk and bring it to a gentle simmer.

5. Add sliced bell peppers, zucchini, mushrooms, and baby corn to the skillet. Cook the veggies for about 5-7 minutes, or until they are soft.

6. Stir in soy sauce and lime juice.

7. Return the cooked tofu to the skillet and toss everything together to coat the tofu and vegetables in the flavorful sauce.

8. Serve the Thai coconut curry over cooked brown rice or quinoa, and garnish with fresh cilantro and sliced red chili if desired.

Mediterranean Tuna Salad Lettuce Wraps

Ingredients:

- 2 cans (5 oz each) tuna, drained
- 1/4 cup chopped cucumber

- 1/4 cup diced red bell pepper
- 1/4 cup diced red onion
- 1/4 cup Kalamata olives, chopped
- 2 tablespoons extra-virgin olive oil
- 1 tablespoon lemon juice
- 1 teaspoon dried oregano
- Salt and pepper to taste
- Butter lettuce leaves (or romaine) for wrapping

Instructions:

1. In a bowl, combine the drained tuna, chopped cucumber, diced red bell pepper, diced red onion, and chopped Kalamata olives.
2. In a separate small bowl, whisk together extra-virgin olive oil, lemon juice, dried oregano, salt, and pepper to make the dressing.
3. When everything is thoroughly blended, drizzle the dressing over the tuna mixture.

4. Spoon the tuna salad into butter lettuce leaves and wrap them up to create lettuce wraps.

5. Serve the Mediterranean tuna salad lettuce wraps for a light and refreshing lunch.

Baked Salmon with Lemon and Dill

Ingredients:

- 2 salmon filets
- 2 tablespoons extra-virgin olive oil
- 1 tablespoon fresh lemon juice
- 1 teaspoon lemon zest
- 2 cloves garlic, minced
- 1 tablespoon fresh dill, chopped
- Salt and pepper to taste
- Sliced lemon and fresh dill sprigs for garnish

Instructions:

1. Preheat your oven to 400°F (200°C).

2. In a small bowl, whisk together the olive oil, lemon juice, lemon zest, minced garlic, chopped dill, salt, and pepper to make the marinade.

3. Place the salmon filets in a baking dish and pour the marinade over them, ensuring they are coated evenly.

4. Let the salmon marinate for about 15-20 minutes to absorb the flavors.

5. The salmon should bake for 12 to 15 minutes in a preheated oven, or until it flakes easily with a fork.

6. Garnish with sliced lemon and fresh dill sprigs before serving

Cauliflower Rice Stir-Fry with Tofu

Ingredients:

- 1 block of firm tofu, cubed
- 1 medium head of cauliflower, grated into rice-like texture
- 1 cup broccoli florets
- 1 cup sliced bell peppers (mixed colors)
- 1 cup sliced carrots
- 1 cup snap peas
- 2 tablespoons sesame oil
- 3 tablespoons of soy sauce (or, for a gluten-free alternative, tamari)
- a teaspoon of rice vinegar
- one tablespoon freshly grated ginger
- 2 minced garlic cloves
- 2 sliced green onions (both the green and white halves)

- Instructions:
- Sesame oil should be heated over medium-high heat in a large pan or wok.

- Cubed tofu should be added and stir-fried until golden and slightly crispy. From the skillet, take out the tofu, and set it aside.
- In the same skillet, add grated cauliflower and stir-fry for 3-4 minutes until it softens slightly.
- Snap peas, sliced carrots, sliced bell peppers, and broccoli florets should all be added to the pan.
- In a small bowl, whisk together soy sauce, rice vinegar, grated fresh ginger, and minced garlic to make the sauce.
- Return the cooked tofu to the skillet and pour the sauce over the vegetables and tofu. Toss everything together until well coated.
- Garnish with sliced green onions before serving.

Lentil and Kale Soup

Ingredients:

- 1 cup washed dry green or brown lentils
- 1 tablespoon olive oil
- 1 onion, chopped
- 2 carrots, diced
- 2 celery stalks, diced
- 3 cloves garlic, minced
- 6 cups vegetable broth
- 1 can (15 oz) diced tomatoes
- 2 cups chopped kale leaves
- 1 teaspoon dried thyme
- 1 teaspoon ground cumin
- Salt and pepper to taste
- Fresh parsley for garnish

Instructions:

1. Olive oil is heated in a large saucepan over a medium flame. Add the diced celery, carrots, and onion. To soften the veggies, sauté for around 5 minutes.

2. Add minced garlic and continue to cook for another minute until fragrant.

3. Pour in the vegetable broth and add the lentils, diced tomatoes, dried thyme, and ground cumin. Bring the soup to a boil.

4. When the lentils are ready, turn the heat down to low, cover the pot, and simmer the soup for 25 to 30 minutes.

5. Cook the chopped kale for a further 5 minutes, stirring occasionally, until it wilts.

6. Add pepperand salt to the soup.

7. Ladle the lentil and kale soup into bowls and garnish with fresh parsley before serving

Spinach and Chickpea Salad with Tahini Dressing

Ingredients:

- 4 cups baby spinach

- chickpeas, drained and rinsed, from one can (15 oz).
- 1/2 cup cherry tomatoes, halved
- 1/2 cucumber, sliced
- 1/4 cup sliced red onion
- 2 tablespoons toasted sesame seeds
- 1/4 cup tahini
- 2 tablespoons lemon juice
- 2 tablespoons water
- 1 clove garlic, minced
- Salt and pepper to taste

Instructions:

1. In a large salad bowl, combine baby spinach, chickpeas, cherry tomatoes, sliced cucumber, and red onion.
2. In a separate small bowl, whisk together tahini, lemon juice, water, minced garlic, salt, and pepper to make the dressing.

3. Drizzle the tahini dressing over the salad and toss everything together until well coated.

Grilled Vegetable Wrap with Hummus

Ingredients:

- 4 whole-grain tortilla wraps
- 1 zucchini, sliced lengthwise
- 1 eggplant, sliced lengthwise
- 1 red bell pepper, sliced into strips
- 1 yellow bell pepper, sliced into strips
- 1 tablespoon olive oil
- 1 teaspoon dried basil
- Salt and pepper to taste
- 1 cup baby spinach
- 1 cup store-bought or homemade hummus
- Fresh mint leaves for garnish (optional)

Instructions:

Over a medium-high flame, preheat your grill or grill pan.

Sliced bell peppers, zucchini, and eggplant and stir with salt, pepper, dried basil, and olive oil in a bowl.

The veggies should be cooked for 3 to 4 minutes on each side, or until grill marks appear and they are soft.

As directed on the packaging, reheat the tortilla wraps.

On each tortilla wrap, spoon 1/4 cup of hummus.

The hummus is topped with baby spinach and grilled veggies.

The tortilla wraps are folded in half after being securely rolled.

For an additional taste boost, garnish with fresh mint leaves.

Quinoa Stuffed Bell Peppers

Ingredients:

- 4 large bell peppers (any color)
- 1 cup cooked quinoa
- 1 cup diced tomatoes (fresh or canned)
- 1 cup diced zucchini
- 1/2 cup diced red onion
- 1/2 cup corn kernels (fresh or frozen)
- 2 cloves garlic, minced
- 1 tablespoon olive oil
- 1 teaspoon ground cumin
- 1/2 teaspoon chili powder
- Salt and pepper to taste
- Fresh cilantro for garnish

Instructions:

1. Preheat your oven to 375°F (190°C).
2. Remove the bell peppers' tops, then scoop out the seeds and membranes.
3. In a large pan, warm the olive oil over medium heat. Red onion dice and minced garlic should be added, and the onion should be cooked until transparent.
4. Add the diced zucchini and simmer for an additional 2 to 3 minutes, or until just softened.
5. Corn kernels, chopped tomatoes, and black beans should all be added to the skillet. Cumin powder, chili powder, salt, and pepper are used as seasonings. To allow the flavors to mingle, cook for 5 minutes.
6. Stir in cooked quinoa and mix everything together.
7. Stuff each bell pepper with the quinoa and vegetable mixture and place them in a baking dish.

CHAPTER 3

DINNER RECIPES

Turmeric-Ginger Roasted Vegetables

1. Ingredients:
- Assorted colorful vegetables (carrots, sweet potatoes, broccoli, bell peppers, zucchini, etc.)
- 2 tablespoons olive oil
- 1 teaspoon ground turmeric
- 1 teaspoon grated fresh ginger
- 1/2 teaspoon ground cumin
- Salt and pepper to taste
- Fresh cilantro or parsley for garnish

Instructions:

1. Put parchment paper on a baking pan and preheat the oven to 400°F (200°C).
2. On the baking sheet, arrange the veggies that have been cut into bite-sized pieces.
3. Olive oil, turmeric, ginger, cumin, salt, and pepper should all be combined in a small bowl.
4. Toss the veggies lightly to cover them equally with the turmeric-ginger combination before drizzling it over them.
5. For 20 to 25 minutes, or until they are soft and just beginning to caramelize, roast the veggies in the preheated oven.
6. Garnish with fresh cilantro or parsley before serving. Enjoy as a vibrant and nutritious main or side dish.

Lemon-Garlic Baked Salmon

7. Ingredients:
- 4 salmon filets

- 2 tablespoons olive oil
- Zest of 1 lemon
- Juice of 1 lemon
- 3 garlic cloves, minced
- 1 teaspoon dried oregano
- Salt and pepper to taste
- Sliced lemon and fresh dill for garnish

Instructions:

1. Preheat the oven to 375°F (190°C) and line a baking dish with parchment paper.
2. Combine the olive oil, lemon zest, lemon juice, minced garlic, dried oregano, salt, and pepper in a small bowl.
3. Make sure the salmon filets are uniformly covered with the lemon-garlic mixture before placing them in the baking dish that has been previously prepared.
4. The salmon should be baked in the preheated oven for 15 to 20 minutes, or until it flakes easily with a fork.

5. Garnish with sliced lemon and fresh dill before serving. Pair this succulent salmon with steamed vegetables or quinoa for a wholesome meal.

Quinoa-Stuffed Bell Peppers

6. Ingredients:
- 4 large bell peppers (any color)
- 1 cup cooked quinoa
- 1 cup cooked black beans
- 1 cup diced tomatoes (canned or fresh)
- 1/2 cup diced red onion
- 1/2 cup corn kernels (fresh or frozen)
- 2 cloves garlic, minced
- 1 teaspoon ground cumin
- 1 teaspoon smoked paprika
- Salt and pepper to taste
- Grated cheddar cheese (optional)

Instructions:

1. Preheat the oven to 375°F (190°C) and lightly grease a baking dish.
2. Bell peppers' tops should be cut off so that the seeds and membranes may be removed. Set apart.
3. Combine the cooked quinoa, black beans, tomatoes, red onion, corn, minced garlic, cumin, smoked paprika, salt, and pepper in a large mixing bowl.
4. Place the bell peppers in the baking dish that has been prepared after stuffing them with the quinoa mixture.
5. Top the filled peppers with shredded cheddar cheese, if preferred.
6. Bake the peppers for 25 to 30 minutes, or until they are soft, with the foil covering the oven dish.
7. Serve the quinoa-stuffed bell peppers as a wholesome and satisfying dinner option

Chicken Stir-Fry with Broccoli and Cashews

1. Ingredients:

- 2 boneless, skinless chicken breasts, thinly sliced
- 2 cups broccoli florets
- 1 red bell pepper, thinly sliced
- 1 cup snow peas
- 1/2 cup raw cashews
- 3 tablespoons low-sodium soy sauce or tamari
- 1 tablespoon honey
- 1 tablespoon rice vinegar
- 1 teaspoon grated fresh ginger
- 2 cloves garlic, minced
- 2 tablespoons olive oil
- Brown or cauliflower rice that has been cooked for serving.
-

Instructions:

1. To create the sauce, combine the rice vinegar, honey, soy sauce (or tamari), grated ginger, and chopped garlic in a small bowl.
2. Heat the olive oil over medium-high heat in a large skillet or wok.
3. When the chicken is cooked through and lightly browned, add it and stir-fry. From the skillet, take out the chicken, and set it aside.
4. If extra oil is required, add it to the same skillet and stir-fry the broccoli, red bell pepper, and snow peas until they are tender-crisp.
5. Add the sauce to the skillet along with the cooked chicken back in it. Combine everything and stir until well hot and coated.
6. Add the raw cashews and stir briefly before removing the skillet from the heat.
7. Serve the flavorful chicken stir-fry over cooked brown rice or cauliflower rice for a balanced and anti-inflammatory dinner.

Lentil and Vegetable Curry

Ingredients:

- 1 cup dried red lentils, rinsed
- 1 tablespoon coconut oil
- 1 large onion, finely chopped
- 2 carrots, diced
- 1 red bell pepper, diced
- 1 tablespoon curry powder
- 1 teaspoon ground turmeric
- 1 teaspoon ground cumin
- 1 can (14 oz) coconut milk
- 1 can (14 oz) diced tomatoes
- 2 cups vegetable broth
- Salt and pepper to taste
- Fresh cilantro for garnish
- Cooked basmati rice or quinoa for serving

Instructions:

1. Heat the coconut oil in a big Dutch oven or saucepan over medium heat.

2. Add the red bell pepper, carrots, and onion, all diced. Until the veggies are just beginning to soften, sauté.
3. Add the ground cumin, ground turmeric, and curry powder. Once the spices are aromatic, cook for one more minute.
4. The pot should now include the rinsed red lentils, coconut milk, chopped tomatoes (with juice), and vegetable broth. Bring the mixture to a boil, then reduce the heat to low, cover the pot, and let it simmer for about 20-25 minutes or until the lentils are tender and the flavors have melded together.
5. Season the lentil and vegetable curry with salt and pepper to taste.
6. Serve the delicious curry over cooked basmati rice or quinoa and garnish with fresh cilantro for an anti-inflammatory dinner that's both hearty and satisfying.

Grilled Chicken and Avocado Salad

1. Ingredients:

- 2 boneless, skinless chicken breasts
- 1 tablespoon olive oil
- 1 teaspoon ground cumin
- Salt and pepper to taste
- Mixed salad greens (spinach, arugula, lettuce, etc.)
- 1 ripe avocado, sliced
- 1/2 cup cherry tomatoes, halved
- 1/4 cup red onion, thinly sliced
- 2 tablespoons toasted pumpkin seeds
- Dressing: 2 tablespoons olive oil, 1 tablespoon balsamic vinegar, 1 teaspoon Dijon mustard, 1 teaspoon honey (optional), salt, and pepper to taste.

Instructions:

1. Preheat the grill or stovetop grill pan over medium-high heat.
2. Rub the chicken breasts with olive oil, ground cumin, salt, and pepper.

3. Grill the chicken for about 5-6 minutes per side or until cooked through. allow it to rest for minutes before slicing.
4. In a large salad bowl, assemble the mixed greens, sliced avocado, halved cherry tomatoes, and red onion.
5. Top the salad with the sliced grilled chicken and toasted pumpkin seeds.
6. In a small bowl, whisk together the dressing ingredients until well combined, and drizzle it over the salad just before serving

Quinoa and Kale Buddha Bowl

1. Ingredients:
- 1 cup cooked quinoa
- 1 cup chopped kale leaves
- 1 cup chickpeas (canned or cooked)
- 1/2 cup grated carrots
- 1/2 cup sliced cucumber
- 1/4 cup sliced radishes

- 1/4 cup crumbled feta cheese (optional)
- Lemon-tahini dressing: 2 tablespoons tahini, 2 tablespoons lemon juice, 2 tablespoons water, 1 clove garlic (minced), salt, and pepper to taste.

Instructions:

1. In a large bowl, combine the cooked quinoa, chopped kale, chickpeas, grated carrots, sliced cucumber, and radishes.
2. If using feta cheese, sprinkle it over the bowl.
3. For the dressing, whisk together the tahini, lemon juice, water, minced garlic, salt, and pepper until smooth. Add more water if needed for a pourable consistency.
4. Drizzle the lemon-tahini dressing over the quinoa and kale Buddha bowl and toss everything together to combine.

Zucchini Noodles with Pesto and Cherry Tomatoes

5. Ingredients:

- 4 medium zucchinis, spiralized into noodles
- 1 cup cherry tomatoes, halved
- 1/4 cup pine nuts, toasted
- Fresh basil leaves for garnish

Pesto Sauce:

- 2 cups fresh basil leaves
- 1/4 cup pine nuts
- 2 cloves garlic
- 1/4 cup grated Parmesan cheese (optional for a non-dairy version)
- 1/2 cup extra-virgin olive oil
- Salt and pepper to taste

Instructions:

1. To make the pesto sauce, combine the basil leaves, pine nuts, garlic, and grated Parmesan cheese (if using) in a food processor. Pulse until coarsely chopped.
2. Add the olive oil in a slow, steady stream while the food processor is running until the pesto is the right consistency. In a large pan, sauté the cherry tomatoes in a little olive oil over medium heat for 1-2 minutes until they soften slightly.
3. Add the zucchini noodles to the pan and sauté for another 2-3 minutes until they are just tender.
4. Toss the zucchini noodles and cherry tomatoes with the prepared pesto sauce until well coated.
5. Serve the zucchini noodles with pesto and cherry tomatoes, topped with toasted pine nuts and fresh basil leaves

Lentil and Vegetable Soup

1. Ingredients:

- 1 cup washed dry green or brown lentils
- 1 tablespoon olive oil
- 1 large onion, chopped
- 2 carrots, diced
- 2 celery stalks, diced
- 2 cloves garlic, minced
- 1 teaspoon ground cumin
- 1 teaspoon ground turmeric
- 1/2 teaspoon ground coriander
- 1/4 teaspoon cayenne pepper (optional, for added heat)
- 6 cups vegetable broth
- 1 can (14 oz) diced tomatoes
- 2 cups chopped spinach or kale
- Salt and pepper to taste
- Fresh parsley for garnish

Instructions:

1. Over medium heat, warm the olive oil in a big saucepan.

2. Add the diced carrots, diced celery, and the chopped onion. Vegetables should be sautéed till tender.

3. Add the ground turmeric, ground coriander, ground cumin, minced garlic, and cayenne pepper (if using) after stirring. Cook the spices for one further minute until they begin to smell.

4. Add the rinsed lentils, vegetable broth, and diced tomatoes (with their juice) to the pot. Bring the mixture to a boil, then reduce the heat to low, cover the pot, and let it simmer for about 20-25 minutes or until the lentils are tender.

5. Stir in the chopped spinach or kale and cook for an additional 5 minutes until the greens wilt.

6. Season the lentil and vegetable soup with salt and pepper to taste.

7. Garnish with fresh parsley before serving this hearty and nourishing soup.

Salmon and Avocado Nori Rolls

8. Ingredients:
- 4 nori sheets
- 2 cups cooked sushi rice (short-grain rice mixed with rice vinegar, sugar, and salt)
- 2 cooked salmon filets, flaked
- 1 ripe avocado, sliced
- 1/2 cucumber, julienned
- Pickled ginger and wasabi for serving (optional)
- Soy sauce or tamari for dipping

Instructions:

1. Place a nori sheet shiny side down on a bamboo sushi rolling mat or a clean, damp kitchen towel.
2. Leave a tiny margin at the top and bottom sides and equally distribute sushi rice over the nori sheet.
3. Arrange the flaked salmon, sliced avocado, and julienned cucumber in the center of the rice.
4. Using the sushi rolling mat or kitchen towel to help you, carefully roll up the nori sheet tightly, starting from the bottom edge. Wet the top border with a little water to seal the roll.
5. Repeat the process with the remaining nori sheets and fillings.
6. Slice the rolls into bite-sized pieces using a sharp knife.
7. Serve the salmon and avocado nori rolls with pickled ginger, wasabi, and soy sauce or tamari for dipping

Mediterranean Quinoa Salad

1. Ingredients:

- 1 cup cooked quinoa
- 1 cup diced cucumber
- 1 cup halved cherry tomatoes
- 1/2 cup chopped Kalamata olives
- 1/4 cup crumbled feta cheese (optional)
- 1/4 cup chopped fresh parsley
- 2 tablespoons extra-virgin olive oil
- 1 tablespoon red wine vinegar
- 1 teaspoon dried oregano
- Salt and pepper to taste

Instructions:

1. In a large bowl, combine the cooked quinoa, diced cucumber, halved cherry tomatoes, chopped Kalamata olives, and chopped parsley.
2. If using feta cheese, add it to the bowl.

3. In a separate small bowl, whisk together the extra-virgin olive oil, red wine vinegar, dried oregano, salt, and pepper to make the dressing.

4. The dressing is prepared by combining the extra virgin olive oil, red wine vinegar, dried oregano, salt, and pepper in a separate small bowl.

Spinach and Chickpea Stuffed Sweet Potato

5. Ingredients:

- 2 large sweet potatoes
- 2 cups fresh baby spinach
- 1/4 cup crumbled goat cheese (optional)
- 2 tablespoons tahini
- 1 tablespoon lemon juice
- 1 clove garlic, minced
- 2 tablespoons water
- Salt and pepper to taste

Instructions:

1. Preheat the oven to 400°F (200°C).
2. Pierce the sweet potatoes with a fork and bake them on a baking sheet for 45-50 minutes or until tender.
3. In the meantime, prepare the filling. In a skillet over medium heat, sauté the chickpeas and baby spinach until the spinach wilts and the chickpeas are heated through.
4. For the tahini sauce, whisk together the tahini, lemon juice, minced garlic, water, salt, and pepper until smooth and pourable.
5. Once the sweet potatoes are done, cut them open lengthwise and gently fluff the flesh with a fork.
6. Spoon the chickpea and spinach mixture into the sweet potatoes, then drizzle the tahini sauce over the top.
7. If using, sprinkle crumbled goat cheese on top before serving

Grilled Vegetable Wrap

1. Ingredients:
- 4 whole-grain or gluten-free wraps
- 1 cup hummus (store-bought or homemade)
- 1 cup mixed grilled vegetables (zucchini, eggplant, bell peppers, etc.)
- 1 cup shredded lettuce or baby spinach
- 1/2 cup sliced red onion
- 1/4 cup sliced Kalamata olives
- Fresh basil leaves for added flavor

Instructions:

1. Set the wraps out on a clean surface.
2. Spread a generous layer of hummus onto each wrap, leaving a small border around the edges.
3. Arrange the grilled vegetables, shredded lettuce, sliced red onion, Kalamata olives,

and fresh basil leaves in the center of each wrap.

4. Fold in the sides of the wrap and then roll it up tightly.

5. Slice the wraps in half and serve immediately, or wrap them in parchment paper for a convenient on-the-go lunch.

Lentil and Roasted Vegetable Salad

6. Ingredients:

- 1 cup cooked green or brown lentils
- 1 cup roasted mixed vegetables (bell peppers, cherry tomatoes, red onion, etc.)
- 1/2 cup crumbled feta cheese (optional)
- 2 tablespoons chopped fresh mint
- 2 tablespoons balsamic vinegar
- 1 tablespoon extra-virgin olive oil
- Salt and pepper to taste

Instructions:

1. In a large bowl, combine the cooked lentils, roasted vegetables, and crumbled feta cheese (if using).
2. Add the chopped fresh mint to the bowl.
3. Drizzle the balsamic vinegar and extra-virgin olive oil over the salad, and toss everything together until well coated.
4. Season with salt and pepper to taste.

Cucumber Avocado Gazpacho

5. Ingredients:

- 2 large cucumbers, peeled and chopped
- 1 ripe avocado, peeled and pitted
- 1 cup plain Greek yogurt (or coconut yogurt for a dairy-free option)
- 1/4 cup fresh cilantro leaves
- 1/4 cup fresh mint leaves
- 1 clove garlic, minced
- 1 tablespoon lime juice
- 1 tablespoon extra-virgin olive oil

- Salt and pepper to taste
- Water or vegetable broth (as needed for desired consistency)

Instructions:

1. In a blender or food processor, combine the chopped cucumbers, avocado, Greek yogurt, cilantro, mint, minced garlic, lime juice, and extra-virgin olive oil.
2. Blend until smooth, adding water or vegetable broth as needed to reach your preferred consistency.
3. Season with salt and pepper to taste.
4. Chill the gazpacho in the refrigerator for at least 30 minutes before serving.
5. Garnish with additional herbs or a drizzle of olive oil, and enjoy the refreshing gazpacho on a warm day

Thai-Inspired Quinoa Salad

1. Ingredients:

- 1 cup cooked quinoa
- 1 cup shredded red cabbage
- 1 cup shredded carrots
- 1 red bell pepper, thinly sliced
- 1/2 cup chopped scallions
- 1/4 cup chopped fresh cilantro
- 1/4 cup chopped fresh mint
- 1/4 cup chopped roasted peanuts
- Dressing: 2 tablespoons lime juice, 1 tablespoon tamari (or soy sauce for non-gluten-free option), 1 tablespoon honey (or maple syrup for a vegan option), 1 tablespoon sesame oil, 1 teaspoon minced one clove of garlic, fresh ginger, salt, and pepper to taste.
-

Instructions:

1. In a large bowl, combine the cooked quinoa, shredded red cabbage, shredded carrots,

sliced red bell pepper, chopped scallions, chopped cilantro, and chopped mint.

2. In a separate small bowl, whisk together the lime juice, tamari, honey, sesame oil, grated ginger, minced garlic, salt, and pepper to make the dressing.

3. Drizzle the dressing over the quinoa salad and toss everything together until well coated.

4. Sprinkle the chopped roasted peanuts on top before serving for added crunch and flavor.

Caprese Chickpea Salad

5. Ingredients:
- 2 cups cooked chickpeas, either from a can or from dried beans.
- 1 cup cherry tomatoes, halved
- 1 cup fresh mozzarella pearls (or diced fresh mozzarella)
- 1/4 cup chopped fresh basil leaves

- Dressing: 2 tablespoons balsamic vinegar, 1 tablespoon extra-virgin olive oil, 1 teaspoon Dijon mustard, salt, and pepper to taste.

Instructions:

1. In a large bowl, combine the cooked chickpeas, halved cherry tomatoes, fresh mozzarella pearls, and chopped basil leaves.
2. In a separate small bowl, whisk together the balsamic vinegar, extra-virgin olive oil, Dijon mustard, salt, and pepper to make the dressing.
3. Drizzle the dressing over the chickpea salad and toss everything together until well combined.
4. Serve the refreshing Caprese chickpea salad as a light and satisfying lunch option

Asian-style Tofu and Vegetable Stir-Fry

1. Ingredients:
- 1 block of firm tofu, cubed
- 2 tablespoons cornstarch
- 2 tablespoons low-sodium soy sauce or tamari
- 1 tablespoon rice vinegar
- 1 tablespoon honey (1 tablespoon maple syrup for vegans)
- one teaspoon of sesame oil
- one tablespoon freshly grated ginger
- 2 minced garlic cloves
- Olive oil, two teaspoons
- 2 cups of mixed veggies, such as carrots, snap peas, broccoli, and bell peppers.
- 2 tablespoons of thinly sliced green onions (scallions)
- Brown rice or cauliflower rice cooked and ready to serve
-

Instructions:

1. In a bowl, toss the cubed tofu with cornstarch until evenly coated.
2. In a separate small bowl, whisk together the soy sauce (or tamari), rice vinegar, honey (or maple syrup), sesame oil, grated ginger, and minced garlic to make the sauce.
3. Warm up the olive oil in a large pan or wok over medium-high heat.
4. The covered tofu should be added to the skillet and stir-fried until crispy and golden.
5. From the skillet, take out the tofu, and set it aside.
6. The mixed veggies should be stir-fried in the same skillet with a little extra oil if necessary until they are crisp-tender.
7. Pour the sauce over the items in the skillet and add the cooked tofu back in. Toss everything together until it is well cooked and coated.
8. Served over cooked brown rice or cauliflower rice, the fragrant tofu and

vegetable stir-fry is a delicious meal. Sliced green onions as a garnish to bring freshness

9.

CHAPTER 4

SNACKS

Turmeric Roasted Chickpeas

1. Ingredients:
   - drained and rinsed 1 can chickpeas
   - 1 tablespoon olive oil
   - 1 teaspoon ground turmeric
   - 1/2 teaspoon ground cumin
   - 1/2 teaspoon paprika
   - Pinch of cayenne pepper (optional)
   - Salt to taste

Instructions:

1. Preheat your oven to 400°F (200°C).

2. Pat dry the chickpeas using a paper towel to remove excess moisture.
3. In a bowl, mix olive oil, turmeric, cumin, paprika, cayenne pepper (if using), and salt.
4. Add the chickpeas to the bowl and toss until evenly coated with the spice mixture.
5. On a baking sheet covered with parchment paper, spread the chickpeas out.
6. Roast in the oven for about 25-30 minutes, or until they become crispy and golden brown.
7. Allow them to cool before storing in an airtight container.

Avocado and Cucumber Salsa

8. Ingredients:
- 1 ripe avocado, diced
- 1 cucumber, diced
- 1 small red onion, finely chopped

- one small jalapeo, with the seeds removed and diced
- 1 tablespoon fresh cilantro, chopped
- Juice of 1 lime
- Salt and pepper to taste

Instructions:

1. In a mixing bowl, combine the diced avocado, cucumber, red onion, jalapeño, and cilantro.
2. Lime juice should be squeezed over the mixture and gently mixed in.
3. Serve with whole-grain tortilla chips or rice crackers.

Baked Sweet Potato Chips

4. Ingredients:

- 2 medium sweet potatoes, washed and thinly sliced
- 1 tablespoon olive oil
- 1 teaspoon ground cinnamon
- 1/2 teaspoon paprika
- Pinch of sea salt

Instructions:

1. Preheat your oven to 375°F (190°C).
2. In a large bowl, toss the sweet potato slices with olive oil, cinnamon, paprika, and sea salt until well-coated.
3. Make sure the slices are evenly spaced out on a baking sheet that has been lined with parchment paper.
4. Bake for about 15-20 minutes, or until the chips are crisp and slightly browned.
5. Allow them to cool completely before serving.

Zucchini and Carrot Fritters

6. Ingredients:

- 1 medium zucchini, grated
- 2 medium carrots, grated
- 1/4 cup chickpea flour (or almond flour)
- 2 cloves garlic, minced
- 1 teaspoon ground cumin
- 1/2 teaspoon ground coriander
- Salt and pepper to taste
- Olive oil for frying

Instructions:

1. In a large bowl, combine the grated zucchini, carrots, chickpea flour, minced garlic, ground cumin, ground coriander, salt, and pepper.
2. Mix well until the ingredients form a thick, cohesive mixture.

3. Olive oil should be warmed up over medium heat in a nonstick pan.
4. Make a tiny patty out of a tablespoon of the ingredients. Spread it out a little bit on the pan.
5. The fritters should be fried for two to three minutes on each side, or until golden brown.
6. Once cooked, transfer them to a plate lined with paper towels to remove excess oil.
7. Serve warm with a dollop of Greek yogurt or tzatziki sauce.

Berry Chia Seed Pudding

8. Ingredients:
- 1 cup mixed berries (blueberries, raspberries, strawberries)
- a single serving of unsweetened almond milk (or other plant-based milk)
- two teaspoons of chia seeds

- 1 tablespoon pure maple syrup (for sweetness; optional)
- 1/2 teaspoon vanilla extract

Instructions:

1. In a blender, combine the mixed berries, almond milk, maple syrup (if using), and vanilla extract.
2. Blend until you have a smooth and creamy mixture.
3. Pour the berry mixture into a glass jar or airtight container.
4. The chia seeds should be thoroughly mixed in.
5. Refrigerate the mixture for at least 4 hours or overnight, allowing the chia seeds to absorb the liquid and thicken the pudding.
6. Before serving, give it a good stir, and if desired, top with a few fresh berries.

Grilled Shrimp Tacos with Avocado Lime Crema

1. Ingredients:

- 1 pound large shrimp, peeled and deveined
- 2 tablespoons olive oil
- 1 teaspoon chili powder
- 1/2 teaspoon ground cumin
- Salt and pepper to taste
- 8 small corn tortillas
- 1 cup shredded purple cabbage
- 1 ripe avocado, sliced
- Fresh cilantro leaves (for garnish)
- Lime wedges (for serving)
- Avocado Lime Crema:
  - 1 ripe avocado
  - 1/2 cup plain Greek yogurt
  - Juice of 1 lime
  - 1 garlic clove, minced
  - Salt and pepper to taste

Instructions:

1. In a bowl, toss the shrimp with olive oil, chili powder, ground cumin, salt, and pepper.

2. Medium-high heat should be used to preheat a grill or grill pan.

3. The shrimp should be grilled for a total of 2 to 3 minutes per side, or until pink and opaque.

4. In a blender or food processor, combine the ingredients for the Avocado Lime Crema. Blend until smooth and creamy.

5. Warm the corn tortillas on the grill for a minute on each side.

6. To assemble the tacos, spread some Avocado Lime Crema on each tortilla.

7. Top with grilled shrimp, shredded purple cabbage, avocado slices, and fresh cilantro leaves.

8. Serve with lime wedges on the side.

Cucumber and Hummus Bites

1. Ingredients:
- 1 large cucumber, sliced into rounds
- 1/2 cup hummus (homemade or store-bought)
- Cherry tomatoes, halved
- Fresh basil leaves
- Black pepper for garnish

Instructions:

1. Lay out the cucumber rounds on a serving platter.
2. Spoon a small amount of hummus onto each cucumber round.
3. Top each round with a halved cherry tomato and a fresh basil leaf.
4. Sprinkle a pinch of black pepper over the bites for added flavor.

Almond Butter Energy Bites

5. Ingredients:

- 1 cup rolled oats
- 1/2 cup almond butter
- 1/3 cup raw honey or maple syrup
- 1/4 cup unsweetened shredded coconut
- 1/4 cup ground flaxseed
- 1/4 cup chopped almonds
- 1 teaspoon vanilla extract
- Pinch of sea salt

Instructions:

1. In a large mixing bowl, combine rolled oats, almond butter, honey or maple syrup, shredded coconut, ground flaxseed, chopped almonds, vanilla extract, and a pinch of sea salt.
2. All the components should be thoroughly combined.

3. To make a bite-sized ball, take a tiny quantity of the mixture and roll it between your palms.

4. Place the energy bites on a parchment-lined tray and refrigerate for about 30 minutes to firm up.

5. Once chilled, transfer the energy bites to an airtight container and keep them refrigerated until ready to snack on.

Roasted Red Pepper and Walnut Dip

6. Ingredients:
- 2 large red bell peppers
- 1/2 cup walnuts
- 2 cloves garlic, minced
- 2 tablespoons extra-virgin olive oil
- 1 tablespoon lemon juice
- 1 teaspoon ground cumin
- 1/2 teaspoon smoked paprika
- Salt and pepper to taste

Instructions:

1. Preheat your oven to broil.
2. Cut the red bell peppers in half, remove the seeds and membranes, and flatten them with your hands.
3. Place the pepper halves on a baking sheet, skin side up, and broil them for about 5-7 minutes or until the skins are charred and blistered.
4. Remove the peppers from the oven, let them cool slightly, and peel off the charred skin.
5. In a food processor, combine the roasted red peppers, walnuts, minced garlic, olive oil, lemon juice, ground cumin, smoked paprika, salt, and pepper.
6. Pulse the mixture until you achieve a smooth and creamy consistency.
7. Transfer the dip to a bowl and serve with raw vegetable sticks or gluten-free crackers

Chia Seed and Mixed Berry Smoothie

8. Ingredients:

- 1 cup mixed berries (strawberries, blueberries, raspberries)
- 1 ripe banana
- a single serving of unsweetened almond milk (or other plant-based milk)
- two teaspoons of chia seeds
- 1 teaspoon maple syrup or honey, if desired, for sweetness
- (Optional) Ice cubes
- Instructions:
- The mixed berries, ripe banana, almond milk, chia seeds, and honey or maple syrup (if used) should all be blended together.
- For a smoothie that is cold, if desired, add additional ice cubes and mix again.
- Place the smoothie in a glass and start eating right away.

Quinoa and Vegetable Salad Cups

1. Ingredients:

- 1 cup cooked quinoa
- 1/2 cup cherry tomatoes, halved
- 1/2 cup cucumber, diced
- 1/4 cup red onion, finely chopped
- 1/4 cup fresh parsley, chopped
- 2 tablespoons extra-virgin olive oil
- 1 tablespoon lemon juice
- 1 teaspoon Dijon mustard
- Salt and pepper to taste
- Lettuce leaves or endive leaves (for serving)

Instructions:

1. Combine the cooked quinoa, cucumber, red onion, cherry tomatoes, and fresh parsley in a big bowl.

2. In a separate small bowl, whisk together the olive oil, lemon juice, Dijon mustard, salt, and pepper to make the dressing.

3. Pour the dressing over the quinoa mixture and toss until everything is well coated.

4. Spoon the quinoa salad into individual lettuce or endive leaves, creating bite-sized cups.

5. Arrange the salad cups on a serving platter and serve immediately.

Spiced Baked Apple Chips

6. Ingredients:

- 2 large apples (use sweet and crisp varieties like Honeycrisp or Fuji)
- 1 teaspoon ground cinnamon
- 1/2 teaspoon ground ginger
- Pinch of nutmeg
- Pinch of sea salt

Instructions:

1. Preheat your oven to 200°F (95°C).

2. Slice the apples thinly using a sharp knife or a mandoline slicer, ensuring uniform thickness for even baking.

3. In a bowl, combine ground cinnamon, ground ginger, nutmeg, and a pinch of sea salt.

4. On a baking sheet covered with parchment paper, spread out the apple slices.

5. Make sure the apple slices are equally covered with the spice mixture before sprinkling it on.

6. Until they are dry and crispy, bake the apple slices in the preheated oven for 1.5 to 2 hours.

7. The chips should be taken out of the oven and allowed to cool fully before being placed in an airtight container.

CHAPTER 5

SMOOTHIES

Tropical Turmeric Delight

1. Ingredients:

- 1 cup coconut milk (or almond milk)
- 1 ripe banana
- 1/2 cup pineapple chunks
- 1/2 cup mango chunks
- 1 tsp turmeric powder (or fresh turmeric root if available)
- 1 tsp grated ginger
- 1 tbsp chia seeds
- a dash of black pepper (to improve the assimilation of turmeric)
- Ice cubes (optional)

Instructions:

1. Add all the ingredients to a blender.
2. Blend until smooth and creamy.
3. Pour into a glass, add ice cubes if desired, and enjoy this refreshing tropical smoothie with a boost of anti-inflammatory benefits.

Berry-Beet Power Smoothie

4. Ingredients:
- 1 cup unsweetened almond milk
- 1/2 cup frozen mixed berries (blueberries, strawberries, raspberries)
- 1 small cooked beetroot, diced
- 1/2 ripe avocado
- 1 tbsp flax seeds
- 1 tsp honey or maple syrup (optional for added sweetness)
- A few mint leaves for garnish (optional)

Instructions:

1. Combine all the ingredients in a blender.
2. Blend until the mixture reaches a smooth and velvety consistency.
3. Pour into a glass, garnish with mint leaves if desired, and enjoy the nutritious and vibrant goodness of this berry-beet power smoothie.

Green Goddess Anti-Inflammatory Smoothie

4. Ingredients:
- 1 cup spinach (or kale, for an extra nutritional punch)
- 1/2 ripe pear
- 1/2 cucumber
- 1/2 avocado
- 1 celery stalk
- 1/2 lemon, juiced
- 1-inch piece of fresh ginger
- 1 cup coconut water
- Ice cubes (optional)

Instructions:

1. Place all the ingredients into a blender.
2. Blend until the mixture turns into a smooth, emerald-green concoction.
3. Pour into a glass, add ice cubes if desired, and relish the refreshing taste of this Green Goddess smoothie, full of anti-inflammatory goodness.

Golden Glow Mango-Turmeric Smoothie

4. Ingredients:
- 1 cup mango chunks
- 1/2 cup Greek yogurt (or dairy-free alternative)
- 1 teaspoon of grated fresh turmeric or turmeric powder
- 1/2 tsp cinnamon
- 1 tbsp honey or maple syrup

- 1/2 cup unsweetened coconut water
- Ice cubes (optional)

Instructions:

1. Combine all the ingredients in a blender.
2. Blend until the mixture achieves a creamy and vibrant texture.
3. Pour into a glass, add ice cubes if desired, and savor the golden goodness of this Mango-Turmeric smoothie, a true delight for your taste buds and inflammation-fighting system.

Berry Spinach Flaxseed Smoothie

1. Ingredients:
- 1 cup fresh spinach
- 1/2 cup frozen mixed berries (strawberries, blueberries, blackberries)

- 1 ripe banana
- 1 tbsp ground flaxseeds
- 1 tbsp almond butter (or any nut butter of your choice)
- 1 cup unsweetened almond milk
- 1 teaspoon honey or maple syrup, if desired, for sweetness
- Ice cubes (optional)

Instructions:

1. Combine all the ingredients in a blender.
2. Blend until the mixture is creamy and well combined.
3. Pour into a glass, add ice cubes if desired, and relish the delightful blend of berries and greens in this Berry Spinach Flaxseed Smoothie, a true nutritional powerhouse.

Creamy Turmeric Avocado Smoothie

4. Ingredients:
- 1 ripe avocado
- 1 cup ripe mango chunks
1. 1 teaspoon of turmeric powder (or freshly grated turmeric)
2. (Or a dairy-free substitute) 1/2 cup plain yogurt
3. 1 tablespoon of honey or agave syrup, tasted,
4. Coconut milk, half a cup
5. Add a dash of black pepper to help the body better absorb turmeric.
6. (Optional) Ice cubes

7. Instructions:
8. In a blender, combine all the ingredients.
9. The ingredients should be smooth and creamy after being blended.
10. Pour into a glass, add ice cubes if desired, and enjoy the creamy goodness of this

Turmeric Avocado Smoothie, packed with anti-inflammatory nutrients

Cherry Almond Spinach Smoothie

11. Ingredients:

- 1 cup fresh spinach
- 1 cup frozen cherries (pitted)
- 1/4 cup almonds (raw or soaked)
- 1/2 ripe banana
- 1 cup unsweetened almond milk
- 1 teaspoon honey or maple syrup, if desired, for sweetness
- 1/2 tsp vanilla extract
- Ice cubes (optional)

Instructions:

1. Combine all the ingredients in a blender.

2. Mixture should be smooth and creamy after blending.

3. Pour into a glass, add ice cubes if desired, and savor the delightful blend of cherries and almonds in this Cherry Almond Spinach Smoothie, providing a burst of anti-inflammatory nutrients.

Cucumber-Avocado Mint Smoothie

4. Ingredients:

- 1/2 cucumber
- 1/2 ripe avocado
- 1 cup baby spinach
- 1 cup coconut water
- A handful of fresh mint leaves
- 1 tbsp chia seeds
- 1 teaspoon honey or agave syrup, taste-tested
- Ice cubes (optional)

Instructions:

1. Place all the ingredients in a blender.
2. Blend until the mixture reaches a creamy and refreshing texture.
3. Pour into a glass, add ice cubes if desired, and relish the cooling sensation of this Cucumber-Avocado Mint Smoothie, loaded with inflammation-fighting properties.

Papaya Turmeric Smoothie

4. Ingredients:
- 1 cup ripe papaya chunks
- 1 small carrot (peeled and diced)
- 1 teaspoon of freshly grated or powdered turmeric
- 1/2 cup orange juice
- 1/2 cup coconut milk
- 1 tbsp fresh lime juice
- A pinch of ground cinnamon

- Ice cubes (optional)

Instructions:

1. Combine all the ingredients in a blender.
2. Blend until the mixture turns into a smooth and vibrant concoction.
3. Pour into a glass, add ice cubes if desired, and enjoy the tropical goodness of this Papaya Turmeric Smoothie, packed with inflammation-reducing nutrients

Blueberry Kale Power Smoothie

4. Ingredients:
- 1 cup fresh kale leaves (stems removed)
- 1 cup frozen blueberries
- 1 ripe banana
- 1/2 cup cucumber (peeled and diced)

- 1 tbsp almond butter (or any nut butter of your choice)
- 1 cup unsweetened almond milk
- 1 teaspoon honey or maple syrup, optional (for sweetness boost)
- (Optional) Ice cubes

- Instructions:
- Blend all the components together according to the instructions.
- Mixture should be smooth and creamy after blending.
- Pour into a glass, add ice cubes if desired, and enjoy the nutritious and antioxidant-rich goodness of this Blueberry Kale Power Smoothie, perfect for reducing inflammation.

Mango-Carrot Turmeric Smoothie

- Ingredients:
- 1 cup ripe mango chunks
- 1 medium carrot (peeled and diced)
- 1/2-inch piece of fresh ginger
- 0.5 teaspoon turmeric powder (or freshly grated turmeric)
- 100 ml of coconut water
- (Or a dairy-free substitute) 1/2 cup plain Greek yogurt
- 1 tbsp chia seeds
- Ice cubes (optional)

Instructions:

1. Combine all the ingredients in a blender.
2. Blend the ingredients up until they're smooth and creamy.
3. Pour into a glass, add ice cubes if desired, and relish the tropical flavors and anti-inflammatory benefits of this Mango-Carrot Turmeric Smoothie.

Raspberry Beet Smoothie Bowl

4. Ingredients:
- 1 small cooked beetroot, diced
- 1 cup frozen raspberries
- (a dairy-free substitute) 1/2 cup plain Greek yogurt
- 1 tbsp almond butter (or any nut butter of your choice)
- 1 tbsp honey or agave syrup (adjust to taste)
- Toppings: Fresh raspberries, sliced almonds, chia seeds, and a sprinkle of cinnamon

Instructions:

1. Place the diced beetroot, frozen raspberries, Greek yogurt, almond butter, and honey/agave syrup in a blender.
2. Blend until the mixture turns smooth and creamy.

3. Pour the smoothie into a bowl and garnish with fresh raspberries, sliced almonds, chia seeds, and a sprinkle of cinnamon.

4. Enjoy this Raspberry Beet Smoothie Bowl, packed with antioxidants and anti-inflammatory properties, as a wholesome and satisfying meal

CHAPTER 6

VEGETABLES RECIPES

Turmeric Roasted Cauliflower

1. Ingredients:

- 1 head cauliflower, cut into florets
- 2 tablespoons olive oil
- 1 teaspoon ground turmeric
- 1/2 teaspoon ground cumin
- 1/2 teaspoon paprika
- Salt and pepper to taste

Instructions:

1. Preheat your oven to 400°F (200°C).

2. In a large mixing bowl, toss the cauliflower florets with olive oil, turmeric, cumin, paprika, salt, and pepper.

3. On a parchment-lined baking sheet, spread the spiced cauliflower out.

4. Roast the cauliflower for 25 to 30 minutes, or until it is soft and gently browned.

5. Serve as a flavorful side dish or add it to salads for an extra kick of anti-inflammatory goodness.

Spinach and Avocado Salad

6. Ingredients:

- 4 cups fresh baby spinach leaves
- 1 ripe avocado, sliced
- 1/4 cup walnuts, chopped
- 1/4 cup dried cranberries
- 2 tablespoons balsamic vinegar
- 1 tablespoon extra-virgin olive oil
- Salt and pepper to taste

Instructions:

1. In a large salad bowl, combine the baby spinach, avocado slices, walnuts, and dried cranberries.
2. Olive oil and balsamic vinegar should be drizzled over the salad.
3. Make sure the ingredients are evenly covered in the dressing by giving them a little toss.
4. Depending on your taste, add salt and pepper to the dish.
5. This refreshing salad is a delightful mix of textures and flavors that's perfect for a light lunch or side dish.

Quinoa Stuffed Bell Peppers

6. Ingredients:
- 4 large bell peppers (any color)
- 1 cup cooked quinoa

- 1 cup black beans, drained and rinsed
- 1 cup diced tomatoes
- 1/2 cup diced red onion
- 1/2 cup diced zucchini
- 1/2 cup diced red bell pepper (from the tops of the bell peppers)
- 2 cloves garlic, minced
- 1 teaspoon ground cumin
- 1 teaspoon chili powder
- 1 tablespoon olive oil
- Salt and pepper to taste
- Fresh cilantro (optional, for garnish)

Instructions:

1. Preheat your oven to 375°F (190°C).
2. Cut the tops off the bell peppers, remove the seeds and membranes, and set aside.
3. Melt the olive oil in a large pan over medium heat. Add the minced garlic, chopped red onion, zucchini, and red bell pepper. to soften, sauté.

4. Add the quinoa that has been cooked, along with the diced tomatoes, black beans, ground cumin, and chili powder. Allow the flavors to combine for a further 3-5 minutes of cooking.
5. Place the quinoa mixture inside each bell pepper before stuffing them.
6. Until the peppers are soft, bake for 25 to 30 minutes.

Roasted Sweet Potato and Kale Salad

Ingredients:

- 2 medium sweet potatoes, peeled and cubed
- 1 bunch of kale, with the stems removed and the leaves shredded into bite-sized pieces.
- 1 tablespoon olive oil
- 1 teaspoon ground turmeric
- 1/2 teaspoon ground cinnamon

- 1/4 cup dried cranberries
- 1/4 cup chopped walnuts
- 2 tablespoons balsamic vinegar
- Salt and pepper to taste

Instructions:

1. Preheat your oven to 400°F (200°C).
2. In a large bowl, toss the sweet potato cubes with olive oil, ground turmeric, ground cinnamon, salt, and pepper.
3. Spread the seasoned sweet potatoes on a baking sheet lined with parchment paper.
4. Roast the sweet potatoes for 20-25 minutes or until they are tender and slightly caramelized.
5. While the sweet potatoes are roasting, lightly massage the torn kale leaves with a drizzle of olive oil to soften them.
6. In a separate small skillet, toast the chopped walnuts over medium heat until fragrant.

7. In a large serving bowl, combine the roasted sweet potatoes, massaged kale, dried cranberries, and toasted walnuts.

8. Drizzle the balsamic vinegar over the salad and toss everything together until well mixed.

9. Serve warm as a hearty and nutritious salad or a satisfying side dish.

Lemon Garlic Broccoli

Ingredients:

- 1 pound broccoli florets
- 2 tablespoons olive oil
- 3 cloves garlic, minced
- Zest of 1 lemon
- 2 tablespoons fresh lemon juice
- 1/4 cup grated Parmesan cheese (optional for a non-vegan version)
- Salt and pepper to taste

Instructions:

1. Steam the broccoli florets until they are tender-crisp.As an alternative, you may blanch them in boiling water for a short period of time.
2. Melt the olive oil in a large pan over medium heat.Add the minced garlic once it becomes aromatic.In the skillet, add the steamed broccoli and stir it with the garlic-infused oil.
3. Toss the broccoli in the freshly squeezed lemon juice to coat.
4. Add salt and pepper to the meal to taste.
5. Sprinkle the lemon zest and grated Parmesan cheese (if using) on top before serving.
6. This lemon garlic broccoli is a zesty and flavorful side dish that compliments a variety of main courses.

Chickpea and Vegetable Curry

Ingredients:

- 1 tablespoon coconut oil
- 1 large onion, chopped
- 3 cloves garlic, minced
- 1 tablespoon grated ginger
- 1 tablespoon curry powder
- 1 teaspoon ground turmeric
- 1 teaspoon ground cumin
- 1 teaspoon paprika
- 1 can chickpeas, drained and rinsed
- 1 cup diced carrots
- 1 cup diced bell peppers (any color)
- 1 cup diced zucchini
- 1 can (14 oz) diced tomatoes
- 1 can (14 oz) coconut milk
- Salt and pepper to taste
- Fresh cilantro, for garnish

Instructions:

1. The coconut oil should be heated over medium heat in a big pan or pot.
2. Add the minced garlic, grated ginger, and onion, all chopped. Once the onions are aromatic and transparent, sauté.
3. Add the curry powder, ground paprika, turmeric, and cumin. The spices should cook for one more minute to toast.
4. Chickpeas, carrots, bell peppers, and zucchini chopped and ready to be added to the pot. To evenly distribute the spice mixture, stir the veggies.
5. Coconut milk and chopped tomatoes with their juice should be added. Add pepper and salt to taste.
6. For 15 to 20 minutes, or until the veggies are soft and the flavors are well-balanced, simmer the curry.
7. Garnish with fresh cilantro before serving.
8. Serve the chickpea and vegetable curry over cooked quinoa or brown rice for a satisfying and filling meal.

Grilled Eggplant and Zucchini Skewers

Ingredients:

- 1 medium eggplant, cut into cubes
- 2 medium zucchini, sliced into rounds
- 1 red onion, cut into chunks
- 1/4 cup balsamic vinegar
- 3 tablespoons olive oil
- 2 cloves garlic, minced
- 1 teaspoon dried oregano
- Salt and pepper to taste
- 30-minute-soaked wooden skewers in water

Instructions:

1. In a bowl, combine balsamic vinegar, olive oil, minced garlic, dried oregano, salt, and pepper to create the marinade.

2. Thread the eggplant cubes, zucchini rounds, and red onion chunks onto the soaked wooden skewers, alternating the vegetables.

3. Place the vegetable skewers in a shallow dish and pour the marinade over them. Make sure all theuniformly coats the veggies.

4. Give the skewers at least 30 minutes to marinate so that the flavors may meld.

5. Medium-high heat should be used to preheat a grill or grill pan.

6. Grill the vegetable skewers for about 10-15 minutes, turning occasionally, until they are tender and slightly charred.

7. Serve the grilled eggplant and zucchini skewers as a delightful and colorful side dish or as a tasty addition to salads

Butternut Squash and Lentil Soup:

Ingredients:

- 1 medium butternut squash, peeled and diced
- 1 cup red lentils, rinsed
- 1 onion, chopped
- 2 cloves garlic, minced
- 1 tablespoon grated fresh ginger
- 1 teaspoon ground turmeric
- 1/2 teaspoon ground cumin
- 4 cups vegetable broth
- 1 can (14 oz) coconut milk
- 2 tablespoons olive oil
- Salt and pepper to taste
- Fresh cilantro or parsley, for garnish

Instructions:

1. Warm the olive oil in a large saucepan over medium heat. When the onion has turned translucent, add it and continue to cook.

2. Add the grated ginger and minced garlic by stirring. Once fragrant, cook for one more minute.

3. Butternut squash dice, red lentils, ground cumin, ground turmeric, and the saucepan. The spices should be well combined with the veggies and lentils.

4. Add the veggie broth, then bring everything to a boil. Once the butternut squash and lentils are cooked, lower the heat to low and allow the mixture simmer for 20 to 25 minutes.

5. After adding the coconut milk, simmer for a further five minutes.

6. Season with salt and pepper to taste.

7. This hearty and comforting butternut squash and lentil soup is an excellent addition to any anti-inflammatory meal plan.

CHAPTER 7

DESSERTS

Berry Chia Seed Pudding

1. Ingredients:

- 1 cup mixed berries (blueberries, raspberries, strawberries)
- 2 tablespoons chia seeds
- 1 cup unsweetened almond milk
- 1 tablespoon pure maple syrup (for sweetness; optional)
- One-half teaspoon of pure vanilla essence
- a dash of cinnamon powder
-
- Instructions:
- The mixed berries, almond milk, maple syrup (if used), and vanilla extract should all be combined in a blender. Mix until emulsified.

- Add the chia seeds after transferring the berry mixture to a bowl.
- Chia seeds will cause the mixture to thicken into a pudding-like consistency, so place the bowl in the refrigerator for at least 2 hours or overnight.
- Add a dash of cinnamon powder to the top just before serving.
- Enjoy this refreshing and nutrient-packed chia seed pudding as a guilt-free dessert!

Baked Cinnamon Apples

- Ingredients:
- 4 apples, preferably Granny Smith or Honeycrisp, of a medium size
- 2 tablespoons coconut oil, melted
- 1 tablespoon pure honey or maple syrup
- 1 teaspoon ground cinnamon
- A pinch of nutmeg (optional)
- A handful of chopped walnuts (for topping)

Instructions:

1. Preheat your oven to 375°F (190°C).

2. Core the apples and slice them into thin rounds or wedges, leaving the peel intact for added fiber and nutrients.

3. In a bowl, mix the melted coconut oil, honey (or maple syrup), ground cinnamon, and nutmeg (if using).

4. Toss the apple slices in the cinnamon mixture until evenly coated.

5. Arrange the coated apple slices on a baking sheet lined with parchment paper.

6. Bake for 15-20 minutes or until the apples are tender and slightly caramelized.

7. Sprinkle chopped walnuts on top before serving. These baked cinnamon apples are perfect on their own or served with a dollop of coconut yogurt.

Turmeric Ginger Cookies

8. Ingredients:

- 1 cup almond flour
- 1/4 cup coconut flour
- 1 teaspoon ground turmeric
- 1/2 teaspoon ground ginger
- 1/4 teaspoon baking soda
- Pinch of salt
- 2 tablespoons coconut oil, melted
- 2 tablespoons pure maple syrup or honey
- 1 teaspoon pure vanilla extract

Instructions:

Set a baking sheet on your oven's 350°F (175°C) rack and preheat the oven.

Almond flour, coconut flour, ground turmeric, ground ginger, baking soda, and salt should all be combined in a bowl.

The dry ingredients should be combined with the melted coconut we oil, maple syrup (or honey), and vanilla essence. Until a dough forms, stir.

Roll the dough into small balls, which you should then place on the baking sheet. Softly flatten each ball with your hands or the back of a spoon.

Bake the rims for 10 to 12 minutes, or until they are golden brown.

Before eating, let the cookies cool on a wire rack. The delicious taste combination and anti-inflammatory properties of these turmeric ginger biscuits are both appealing.

Avocado Chocolate Mousse

1. Ingredients:
- 2 ripe avocados
- 1/4 cup unsweetened cocoa powder
- 1/4 cup pure maple syrup or honey
- 1 teaspoon pure vanilla extract
- Pinch of salt
- Fresh berries (for garnish)

Instructions:

1. Place the avocados' flesh in a food processor or blender.
2. The avocados should be mixed with the cocoa powder, maple syrup (or honey), vanilla essence, and a dash of salt.
3. Blend until the mixture is creamy and smooth, pausing occasionally to scrape the sides.
4. Transfer the chocolate mousse to individual serving dishes or a large bowl.
5. Refrigerate for at least 30 minutes before serving to allow the flavors to meld and the mousse to chill.
6. Garnish with fresh berries just before serving. This avocado chocolate mousse is a luscious and healthy treat!

Almond Butter and Banana Bites

7. Ingredients:

- 2 ripe bananas, sliced into rounds
- 2 tablespoons almond butter
- Unsweetened shredded coconut (optional, for topping)
- Dark chocolate chips (optional, for topping)

Instructions:

1. Lay the banana rounds on a plate or tray.
2. Each slice of banana should have a tiny amount of almond butter on it.
3. Optionally, sprinkle shredded coconut and dark chocolate chips on top for added texture and flavor.
4. Refrigerate the banana bites for 10-15 minutes before serving. These delightful almond butter and banana bites offer a satisfying combination of sweet and nutty flavors.

Coconut Blueberry Popsicles

6. Ingredients:

- 1 cup coconut milk (full-fat, canned)
- 1 cup fresh or frozen blueberries
- 1 tablespoon pure honey or maple syrup
- 1 teaspoon pure vanilla extract
- Zest of half a lemon (optional)

Instructions:

1. In a blender, combine the coconut milk, blueberries, honey (or maple syrup), and vanilla extract.
2. Optionally, add the lemon zest for a zesty twist to the popsicles.
3. Blend until smooth and well combined.
4. Popsicle sticks should be inserted into each mold once the mixture has been poured into them.

5. Make sure the popsicles are thoroughly frozen by freezing them for at least four hours.
6. Run the popsicle molds through some warm water to help the popsicles come out.
7. Enjoy these refreshing and antioxidant-rich coconut blueberry popsicles as a cool treat

Mango Turmeric Sorbet

1. Ingredients:
- 2 ripe mangoes, peeled and diced
- 1 teaspoon ground turmeric
- 2 tablespoons pure honey or maple syrup
- 1 tablespoon fresh lime juice
- 1/2 cup water

Instructions:

1. In a blender, combine the diced mangoes, ground turmeric, honey (or maple syrup), and lime juice.
2. In order to get the correct consistency, gradually add the water.
3. Blend the ingredients until it's creamy and smooth.
4. To stop ice crystals from forming, transfer the sorbet mixture to a shallow dish, cover it with plastic wrap, and make sure the plastic wrap contacts the sorbet's surface.
5. For at least 3 to 4 hours, or until the sorbet is solid, freeze it.
6. Freeze the sorbet for at least 3-4 hours, or until firm.
7. Scoop the sorbet into serving bowls and garnish with fresh mint leaves or lime zest. This mango turmeric sorbet is a delightful and tropical treat with anti-inflammatory benefits.

Cinnamon Baked Pears

8. Ingredients:

- 4 ripe pears, halved and cored
- 1 tablespoon coconut oil, melted
- 2 tablespoons pure honey or maple syrup
- 1 teaspoon ground cinnamon
- A handful of chopped pecans or almonds (optional)

Instructions:

1. A baking dish should be lined with parchment paper and your oven should be preheated to 375°F (190°C).
2. Place the pear halves, cut side up, in the baking dish.
3. In a small bowl, mix the melted coconut oil, honey (or maple syrup), and ground cinnamon.
4. Drizzle the cinnamon mixture over the pear halves, making sure they are well coated.
5. Optionally, sprinkle chopped pecans or almonds on top for added crunch and flavor.

6. Bake the pears for 25-30 minutes, or until they are tender and slightly caramelized.

7. Allow the baked pears to cool slightly before serving. These cinnamon baked pears are a warm and comforting dessert that pairs perfectly with a scoop of dairy-free vanilla ice cream

Recipe index

Breakfast

a) Turmeric Smoothie Bowl

Ingredients:

- 1 cup frozen mixed berries
- 1 ripe banana
- 1 tsp turmeric powder
- 1/2 cup almond milk
- 1 tbsp chia seeds
- Toppings: sliced kiwi, shredded coconut, and a sprinkle of cinnamon

b) Avocado and Spinach Omelet

Ingredients:

- 3 eggs (or plant-based alternative)
- 1/4 cup fresh spinach
- 1/4 avocado, sliced
- 1 tbsp olive oil
- Salt and pepper to taste

2. Lunch:

a) Grilled Salmon Salad

Ingredients:

- 4 oz grilled salmon
- Mixed greens (kale, arugula, spinach)
- 1/4 cup cherry tomatoes, halved
- 1/4 cup cucumber, sliced
- 1/4 cup sliced bell peppers
- Lemon-tahini dressing: 1 tbsp tahini, 2 tbsp lemon juice, 1 tsp honey, water (to desired consistency)

b) Quinoa and Roasted Vegetable Bowl

Ingredients:

- 1 cup cooked quinoa
- Roasted vegetables (sweet potatoes, zucchini, red onions)
- 1/4 cup chickpeas
- Fresh parsley
- Drizzle of balsamic vinegar and olive oil

3. Dinner:

a) Turmeric-Ginger Baked Chicken

Ingredients:

- 2 chicken breasts
- 1-inch piece of ginger, grated
- 1 tsp turmeric powder
- 2 cloves garlic, minced
- 2 tbsp coconut aminos
- 1 tbsp olive oil

b) Cauliflower Rice Stir-Fry:

Ingredients:

- 2 cups cauliflower rice
- Broccoli, carrots, and snap peas make up one cup of mixed veggies.
- 1/4 cup diced tofu or lean protein of choice
- 2 tbsp low-sodium soy sauce (or tamari for gluten-free option)
- 1 tsp sesame oil
- Optional toppings: sesame seeds, sliced green onions
4. Snacks:

a) Almond Butter Apple Slices

Ingredients:

- 1 medium apple, sliced

- 2 tbsp almond butter
- A sprinkle of ground cinnamon

b) Spiced Chickpea Nuts

Ingredients:

- 1 cup cooked chickpeas
- 1 tsp olive oil
- 1/2 tsp ground cumin
- 1/2 tsp smoked paprika
- 1/4 tsp cayenne pepper (adjust to taste)
- Salt to taste
5. Desserts:

a) Chia Seed Pudding

Ingredients:

- 1/4 cup chia seeds

- 1 cup coconut milk
- 1 tsp pure maple syrup
- Fresh berries for topping

b) Baked Cinnamon-Pear Crisp:

Ingredients:

- 2 ripe pears, sliced
- 1/2 cup rolled oats
- 1/4 cup almond flour
- 1/4 cup chopped walnuts
- 1 tbsp coconut oil
- 1 tsp ground cinnamon
- 1 tbsp honey

Remember, the key to the anti-inflammatory diet is to focus on whole foods, plenty of fruits and vegetables, healthy fats, and lean proteins.

CONCLUSION

the impact of an inflammatory diet on human health is undeniable and warrants serious consideration. The evidence presented throughout this discussion emphasizes the pivotal role that dietary choices play in shaping our well-being and the potential consequences of consuming an inflammatory diet.

Numerous scientific studies have linked an inflammatory diet to a myriad of health issues, ranging from chronic conditions like cardiovascular diseases, obesity, and diabetes, to autoimmune disorders and even certain cancers. These findings underscore the urgent need for individuals to take proactive steps in reassessing their dietary habits to reduce inflammation and promote overall health.

While it is essential to acknowledge that inflammation is a natural and necessary response for the body's defense mechanism, chronic and excessive inflammation can be detrimental to our health. An inflammatory diet, characterized by excessive consumption of processed foods, sugary beverages, refined carbohydrates, and unhealthy fats, perpetuates a state of chronic inflammation in the body, disrupting its balance and harmony.

To combat the adverse effects of an inflammatory diet, adopting an anti-inflammatory dietary approach is highly recommended. This entails incorporating more whole foods, such as fruits, vegetables, whole grains, nuts, seeds, and fatty fish, which are rich in antioxidants, vitamins, minerals, and omega-3 fatty acids. These nutrients have been shown to have anti-inflammatory properties, helping to quell inflammation and support overall wellness.

Additionally, reducing the intake of processed foods, sugary snacks, and excessive red meat can further aid in mitigating inflammation. Instead, embracing a balanced and diverse diet that prioritizes whole and unprocessed foods can pave the way for better health outcomes.

Education and awareness about the inflammatory potential of certain foods are vital in empowering individuals to make informed dietary choices. Healthcare professionals, policymakers, and the food industry must work collaboratively to promote healthier food options, provide accessible nutritional education, and implement strategies to combat the prevalence of inflammatory diets.

Printed in Great Britain
by Amazon

41644509R00099